But of Power, and of Love, and of a Sound Mind

Battling Fear in a Troubled World

Dirk Webb

Other Books by Dirk Webb

A Warm Summer's Day

The Next Summer's Day

The Adventures of Mousey Carter McCloud

The Amazing City of Arbella Lamore

Mousey Carter McCloud, Private Eye

Hearing Eyes, Talking Hands: A Child's Questions About Deafness

What Color am I Today?

The Prettiest Psalm: The Art of Judith Webb

Kings and Things: Stories of the Old Testament

The Art of Hope: Illustrated by Judith Webb

Scoopy and Brian

What's a Grampa?

It's Time to Move

We're Moving

www.dirkwebbandfriends.com

Printed in the United States of America, 2021

ISBN: 9798716445284

A Little About this Book

Normally, I write children's books and love doing it. Recently, I felt an urgency I'd never felt before.

A dear friend of mine was facing an important surgery with no way to know the outcome. She mentioned that she would like to have prayer before the operation and I gladly agreed to pray for her.

As we "gathered" around her on a Zoom call, I felt the Lord directing to pray for her using 2 Timothy 1:7:

"For God hath not given us the spirit of fear, but of power, and of love, and of a sound mind."

During the weeks after that prayer session, thoughts and ideas on that passage kept dropping into my mind. I decided to write them down.

I hope these thoughts help you as much as they did me.

Dirk—2021

...But of Power, Love and a Sound Mind

2 Timothy 1:7 – "For God has not given us the spirit of fear, but of power, and of a sound mind." (NKJV)

Introduction

The world we live in today threatens our peace of mind. Between racial and cultural strife, economic pressures, government and election controversies, family struggles and a myriad of other challenges, we are faced with worries on top of worries.

The American population seems awash in diabetes, sexual diseases, obesity, divorce, pornography, child abuse and violence. As a result, we suffer from sleepless nights, shattered relationships and fear of the unknown.

We try self-help books and videos, chants and mantras and all kinds of self-comfort. We are seeking counseling in record numbers, setting new highs in health care expenditures, and homicide rates that leave us bewildered and devastated.

Even those who profess to be "born again" Christians find themselves enveloped in doubt and confusion to the point of wondering if everything they've been taught since Sunday School is not all as it was presented.

We look back on previous years and even decades fondly and remember them as "the good old days" and long for a simpler time when life appeared to be without worry.

Father might have "known best" in the old days, but today, Father may not even be present. We may look back on the hit music of our high school days and wonder where time went. We may even look in the mirror and try to understand when the lines, wrinkles and graying hair appeared.

Sadly, if someone were to mention church, religion or Jesus Christ, many times the speaker is looked on with derision, suspicion or actual hostility. Yet, for all our seeming disgust about biblical principles or the message of Christ, we have no better solution for a society that claims to be "enlightened" but is clearly in crisis.

The scripture above, 2 Timothy 1:7, makes the claim that "God hath not given us the spirit of fear, but of power, and of love, and of a sound mind." In a world that is so willing to try anything and everything to meet its needs, why have we abandoned such a positive message? How can we make sense of a world where everything we've been told is wrong is now said to be right, and everything that we've been told is right is now said to be wrong?

John writes to us in chapter 10, verse 10 that Jesus said, "the thief comes only in order to steal, kill and destroy. I came that they may have and enjoy life, and have it in abundance (to the full, till it overflows".) Amazingly, so many believers are asking themselves, "where is this abundant life that I am supposed to be having? Why am I struggling with my faith? Why am I fearful when I am supposed to be an overcomer?"

Why was Paul writing to Timothy on this subject?

The Apostle Paul recognized great attributes in his young protégé, Timothy. Earlier in Chapter 1 Paul tells Timothy that he was "filled with joy" when he remembered the "genuine faith that is in you." Paul goes on to note that Timothy's faith had been taught to him from an early age by his grandmother and mother.

Paul, feeling the urge to mentor Timothy, instructs him to "stir up the gift of God which is in you through the laying on of my hands." He further encourages Timothy saying, "For God has not given us a spirit of fear, but of power, and of love and of a sound mind." (NKJV)

Today, we have over 2,000 years of church experience complete with the teachings of the Apostles, early Church Fathers, and volumes of works that have informed, encouraged and trained believers. In Paul and Timothy's time, Christianity was so new that boldness in the face of persecution was a necessity in delivering the Gospel message.

Persecution took many different forms including bestial brutality, the loss of family, the loss of income, and the loss of reputation. For young Timothy, being charged with helping to spread the Word was undoubtedly a daunting task.

Paul reminds him in verse 12, "For this reason I also suffer these things; nevertheless, I am not ashamed, for I know whom I have believed and am persuaded that He is able to keep what I have committed to Him until that Day." (NKJV)

All these centuries later, we are encouraged by those words. They have been the text of countless sermons, devotionals and even hymns.

There is a question that we must face today: is this writing to Timothy that came so eloquently from Paul's pen applicable today? If so, how do we apply it? Why did he select three subjects that are so loaded with meaning; power, love and soundness of mind.

Before we dig into this verse further, we're reminded that later in the same writing to Timothy the Apostle reminds us all that:

All Scripture *is* given by inspiration of God, and *is* profitable for doctrine, for reproof, for correction, for instruction in righteousness, that the man of God may be complete, thoroughly equipped for every good work. (2 Timothy 3:6-17, NKJV)

In other words, if we believe that God's Word never changes. If we believe that it is as important in our lives today as when it was written. And, if we believe that the bible is written through the inspiration of the Holy Spirit and not just the whims of a collection of writers, then we must believe that Paul's gentle encouragement to Timothy is absolutely God breathed and life changing today.

Fear

*"For God hath not given us the **Spirit of Fear**, but of Power, and of Love, and of a sound mind."*

Fear. There is no emotion that evokes such a wide range of reactions in us. Many of us associate fear with an unrelenting dread of the unknown or a gnawing certainty that only the worst will come upon us. Job remarked in 3:25, "For the thing which I greatly feared is come upon me."

God gave us a healthy dose of fear to keep us from danger. We are repulsed by altitude, extreme heat, prolonged exposure to bitter cold, and reptiles. In most cases, fear reminds us to take care to preserve ourselves from injury and even death.

When put in spiritual terms, Paul quickly wrote to Timothy that, "God has not given us the spirit of fear…" Immediately the Apostle defines this type of fear as a spirit indicating that, in this case, fear causes an emotional reaction that can lead to anxiety, depression and a paralysis of mind and body.

Fear is in the root of nearly every aspect of unbelief. Yet Jesus declared that "God did not send His Son into the world to condemn the world." We sometimes look down on those who struggle in faith and belief and fail to look beyond the outward appearances to understand that fear drives many of those expressions.

Often marital strife may be an expression of one's fear of domination by the other, one's fear of the disintegration of the family, or even a fear of living their life alone. A person who spends themselves into financial hardship may have endured a deprived childhood and fears returning to having nothing. The e exact opposite is possible where someone who lived through severe deprivation saves every cent vowing never to be poor again.

In Mark Chapter 9, a man brought his son to Jesus who was possessed by a spirit that rendered him speechless. The spirit caused the young man to have seizures, foaming at the mouth, and gnashing of teeth.

When Jesus asked how long his son had been in that condition, the anguished father replied, "from childhood." He further related experiences of watching as the spirit caused him to be thrown into fire or water in order to kill him.

He appealed to Jesus, "If you can do anything, take pity on us and help us."

Jesus, as always, was moved with compassion by the human suffering displayed before Him said, "Everything is possible for one who believes."

The father, partly in desperation but with a glimmer of hope exclaimed, "I do believe, help me overcome my unbelief." At that point, Jesus took command of that spirit and cast it out.

Does this mean that everyone who suffers is possessed? Absolutely not. But fear is the greatest tool the enemy uses to keep us from the promises of God. This father recognized his fear but also understood that it was Jesus who stood before him and that He could overcome any fear. For the Father, faith said, "I believe that Jesus can do all He says." Fear was saying, "what if Jesus can't help me and my son dies?"

What about us? What do we think as Jesus stands before us?

"I believe, but what if God is not enough? What if this sickness kills me?"

"I believe, but what if God is not enough? I could go bankrupt and lose everything."

"I believe, but what if God is not enough? My children and family may turn against me."

Just like the father in the book of Mark, our answer must always be, "Lord, I believe, help my unbelief."

God has not given us the spirit of fear

If we have determined that fear is, after all, a spirit, Paul declares immediately that it is not from God. If the spirit of fear doesn't come from God there is only one other source: the enemy. Often, we seem to confuse the two forces surrounding us.

When bad things happen to us we think they come from God for a myriad of reasons.

"This is a punishment for all the bad things I've done."

"If God is so big and controls everything, He could stop this from happening."

"God just doesn't care about me. I'm not important to Him."

First, James 1:17 reminds us that "every good and perfect gift is from above, coming down from the Father of the heavenly lights who does not change like shifting shadows." (NIV) Our modern minds have forgotten the simple truth that "God is good all the time, and all the time God is good."

We also need to understand that God is not vengeful. He doesn't sit in heaven waiting for the next opportunity to "teach us a lesson." Psalm 103:12 says that "as far as the east is from the west so far has He removed our transgressions from us."

Basically, once we put our past under the blood of Jesus, God has this wonderful case of amnesia. He doesn't remember our transgressions so, in His mind, there's nothing to punish or take vengeance for."

Because of the world's view today over the source of good versus evil, God versus Satan, we are constantly in a state of confusion. 1 Corinthians 14:33 tells us that "God is not the author of confusion, but of peace..." (KJV) So, if God is not the author of confusion, and is not vengeful, then it is impossible for God to be the source of fear.

Finally, if God is not vengeful and is not the author of confusion, then we must also accept that God never changes. Jesus told us all that, "Heaven and earth will pass away but My words, will by no means pass away." (Matthew 24:35) If we assume then that God never changes, never has, never will, then we can also assume that He will never be vengeful and will never cause us confusion.

If fear is not from God, then where?

There can only be one other source of fear; the enemy. Is that too simplistic of a conclusion? What about the human element? Can fear be caused by things we conjure up in our own minds?

When we strip the spiritual world to its most basic elements we remember that "In the beginning God created the heaven and the earth. Now the earth was formless and empty, darkness was over the surface of the deep, and the Spirit of God was hovering over the waters." (Genesis 1:1) (NIV)

From the very first verse, of the very first chapter, of the very first book of the Bible we are introduced to the spirit world; in this case, the very Spirit of God. Before humans, before any other creation, God's Spirit was already making His presence felt.

To take it even further, John 1 explains "In the beginning was the Word, and the Word was with God, and the Word was God. He was with God in the beginning. Through Him all things were made; without Him nothing was made that has been made." (John 1: 1-3 NIV) The truth of the matter is, the Father, the Son and the Spirit were all present before any creation was ever attempted.

The first reference to an evil entity occurs in the Book of Genesis as well. In the guise of a serpent, Satan first appears to Adam and Eve convincing them to eat from the tree." Immediately the serpent

contradicts God by stating, "Did God really say, '**You must not eat from any tree in the garden**?'"

In the previous chapter God said to Adam, "And the LORD God commanded the man, "**You are free to eat from any tree in the garden**; but you must not eat from the tree of the knowledge of good and evil, for when you eat from it you will certainly die." (Genesis 2:16-17 NIV)

If we look closer at the argument that Satan poses to Adam and Eve we notice that his response was quite different from God's instructions. God told them they could eat from any tree in the garden except for the tree of the knowledge of good and evil. Notice Satan's distortion as mentioned above, "Did God really say, 'You must not eat from any tree in the garden?'"

Jesus gave us the true attributes of Satan in John 8:44 "...He was a murderer from the beginning, not holding the truth, for there is no truth in him. When he lies, he speaks his native language, for he is a liar and the father of lies." (NIV)

If we go back to Luke 10:18, Jesus refers to that same period before Adam and Eve when he says, "I saw Satan fall like lightning from heaven." The essence here is that Jesus knew all about Satan, that he was a murderer and liar from the beginning.

We've already mentioned that the Spirit of God was present at the beginning, the Word, Jesus, was present at the beginning and they were intimately acquainted with Satan's characteristics long before Adam and Eve came to be.

We can safely conclude then that if God has not given us the spirit of fear there is one logical source; Satan himself. Could we possibly fear anyone who is the essence of love, joy, peace, forbearance, kindness, goodness, faithfulness, gentleness and self-control; all listed as fruits of that same Spirit. (Galatians 5:22-23)

Conversely, we can easily reconcile fear with a someone who is the opposite of all those attributes and who is a murderer first, and the source of all lies.

Fear and our imagination

To be clear, we cannot faithfully say that every amount of fear and unbelief is originated in the spirit world. The father of the son Jesus healed exclaimed, "Lord, I believe. Help my unbelief." He was plainly acknowledging that he was struggling to believe and asking Jesus to come to his rescue.

Paul, in another writing to the church in Corinth in 2 Corinthians, Chapter 10, referred to the human difficulties with faith and unbelief.

> *³ For though we walk in the flesh, we do not war after the flesh:*
> *⁴ (For the weapons of our warfare are not carnal, but mighty through God to the pulling down of strong holds;)*

The Apostle makes it clear that we walk in the flesh. Even though our opponents are in the spiritual world, the tools we have been given are not carnal, or physical, but they are spiritual weapons given to us to wage spiritual warfare.

He then reminds his readers that they are to "cast down imaginations" or any teaching, theories, or revelations that are in direct conflict with the Word of God. Paul admonishes us to bring into captivity, or control every thought making it line up with the teachings of Jesus.

Paul is encouraging us to be well grounded in the Word of God and able to "rightly divide the word of truth." But, he is also showing us that some of our difficulties come from what we are feeding our own spirit through our mind.

The language Paul uses in these verses is a definite reminder that the battle for our mind is real and those fights are ones that Satan particular tries to use to his advantage. Image evoking words such as "casting down" and "bringing into captivity" help us know that this is a war. We must always be on guard against allowing the enemy an open door into our lives; especially our thoughts.

Today, we are bombarded with content contrary to the Word of God and more simply, dangerous to our own peace of mind. News organizations drill us constantly with articles designed to scare us, anger us and deprive us of calm nerves.

If, then, Satan is a murderer and a liar, it is very easy to perceive that the warfare for our mind would include ideas, images and meditations that would bring an avalanche of fear intended to bury us, our families, our marriages and everything we hold dear including our peace of mind.

Paul uses additional war-like imagery when, in Ephesians 6:12 he warns, **"For we wrestle not** against flesh and blood, but against principalities, against powers, against the rulers of the darkness of this world, against spiritual wickedness in high places."

At first glance it would be easy to find a fight against that list of foes absolutely unwinnable. Yet, as seen above, the weapons of our warfare are not physical but they are mighty through God for the pulling down of strongholds. The battle is ours for the claiming through Jesus.

Fear versus Fact

Often our fears are simply rooted in a lack of knowledge or a "fear of the unknown." We may base our concerns on assumption or second-hand information. As children, we are afraid of the dark. An adult in our lives may have explained to us repeatedly that nothing changed from the time we had the lights on until the second when the lights were turned off. But to our young minds, visions of monsters and other such beings would come to mind immediately.

As adults, the higher amount of uncertainty that exists in our lives, the more anxiety and fear we feel. Perhaps the economy took a turn for the worst and we assume that our jobs or businesses are in jeopardy.   Many of us are concerned as we age that our health will deteriorate and we feel deep anxiety over our future. Hosea

received a word from God that, "my people are destroyed for a lack of knowledge..." (4:6) He goes on to write that God's people had actually rejected knowledge. The rejection of the Word of God and its advice contributes to our fears.

At other times our fears are seated in past experiences. For many of us who come from broken families, a lingering fear accompanies us into our own marriage and family life. If we have spent our lives running from God, committing a variety of sins, we may bring that "baggage" along with us. We find ourselves wrestling with guilt, confusion and turmoil. Before we realize it, we expect that everyone lives this way.

If we have cheated on a spouse, we fear that they will do they same. If we have been a victim of abuse, we may fear that the cycle may continue in our family for generations to come. Our fears become deeply embedded in our own disappointments; with family and friends, business associates and, most devastating of all, with ourselves.

If we have been unethical or experienced scandal in our professional lives, we may live with the fear of being discovered and becoming front page news. Our fear can lead to sleepless nights, extraordinary stress and physical issues that can compound the anxiety we already feel.

Fear and Stress Management

Go to any bookstore, (that term is almost obsolete now) or online book seller and we will find title after title of self-help books claiming to have the magic key to dissolving stress in our lives. From exercise, to diet, to meditation, to medication, we are given a myriad of recipes that will give us a good night's sleep or make our nauseous stomachs calm down.

Unfortunately, Christians seem to be just as prone to fear, anxiety and depression as any other group. Our preachers combine for hours of sermons on handling stress. Christian counselors crank out page upon page of scripture-based wisdom.

This book isn't intended to answer those questions or solve those problems. Our purpose is to provide you with some thought-provoking ideas and suggestions and to let you know the most important point of all:

You are not alone. Many of us have been where you are. More importantly, God is with each of us.

Power

*"For God hath not given us the Spirit of Fear, **but of Power**, and of Love, and of a sound mind."*

We've talked a lot about fear. Our scripture, "For God has not given us a spirit of fear, but of power, and of love and of a sound mind," has some similarities to an algebraic equation. We were taught that "a+b=c" and that to solve for "c" we could move the variables from one side of the equal sign to the other but we had to balance it out with an opposite move from the other.

In accounting we learn that assets = liabilities + equity. Anything we do on the asset side of the equal sign must have an opposite entry on the other side of the equal sign.

So, with our text, if God has not given us the spirit of fear, or, if that fear is to be removed, it must be replaced by something else.

Paul says that the first value on that side of the equation is "Power."

In our previous discussion we mentioned that in Genesis 1:1 the Spirit of God was already hovering over the deep, poised to perform whatever came from the mouth of God. Immediately, in verse 2 we are witnesses to the unbelievable power of God.

[3] And God said, "Let there be light," and there was light. That simple sentence vastly understates the surge of creative power when, from a vast sea of darkness, light and all of its energy came to being from His breath.

In Romans 8:11, Paul writes these words, "But if the Spirit of Him that raised up Jesus from the dead dwell in you, He that raised up Christ from the dead shall also quicken your mortal bodies by His Spirit that dwelleth in you. (AKJV)

Think about that for just a second. Can you imagine the power that was generated to raise Jesus from the dead; to bring life back into a body that had ceased to breathe? Can you imagine that very second when Jesus' eyes flashed open and a burst of air entered in His lungs? Paul tells us that the very same power through the Spirit of God that shocked Jesus' heart into rhythm again, can dwell in you causing the same explosive energy to course through your body.

The good news here is that the very Power of God, the creator of heaven and earth, is available to us. If we have that power at our disposal, how can fear possibly exist?

The Power of the Church

Some people, even Christians, sometimes moan at the thought of regular church attendance. We are guilty at times of wanting to rest a bit more on the weekend, or we're concerned that the church is only after our money (we'll talk more about that later.) In fact, the Church was anointed to be the first refuge from the onslaughts of the enemy.

Paul noted the role of the Church in the daily battle against fear. Romans 10:17 reminds us, "So faith comes by hearing, and hearing by the word of God." Paul doesn't say, "Faith comes through self-help books" or "Faith comes by listening to Christian music." Those two items have their place, but we are specifically admonished to listen to the word of God."

There is nothing more influential to our Christian life and the building of power that to be a part of a dynamic, bible-believing, missions driven Church.

Hebrews 10:25 instructs "Not forsaking the assembling of ourselves together, as the manner of some is; but exhorting one another: and so much the more, as ye see the day approaching." (KJV) If we read a little closer, the reason for regular church attendance is to exhort one another. Exhort, in this case, means to encourage or even to incite each other to greater action.

I've often compared church attendance to trying to lose weight by yourself. You can do it, but it sure is easier when you're part of a group effort. We are at church together to not only worship our Lord, but to build each other up in the faith which immediate translates into power for our lives.

We can supplement our church attendance with wonderful preaching, teaching and worship available to us through many Christian networks, YouTube videos, and countless podcasts. But, being together with like minded believers is so important.

An active faith also requires doing. Where else but your local church will you find a full complement of bible centered activities and events where you can volunteer? As you pour yourself into the lives of others, you can't help but feel that creative power of God as you put your faith into action.

Joining a powerful church body is vital to recognizing and fighting the lies of the enemy that lead to fear.

The Power of the Word

In addition to our church attendance, we need to spend time in God's word. If you attended Sunday School you might have been admonished to "read the bible" during the week. One of the problems was, we weren't always told just where to read.

Perhaps you've tried to start at the New Testament with Matthew Chapter 1 and got lost in the long list of "begats." Maybe you worked through Genesis and Exodus only to get bogged down in the measurements of the temple and the intricacies of the law as it was delivered to Israel.

I suggest that you start with the Book of John. The entire core of our faith lies in understanding that God loved us so much that He gave "His only begotten son, that whosoever believeth on Him should not perish but have everlasting life." (John 3:16)

The Book of John is a treasure trove of Jesus' love for us. He prays for you in Chapter 17. He promises you an everlasting home with Him in John 14. If you're a veteran Christian you may be amazed as you re-read this beautiful writing that new aspects of His love that you never noticed before now stand out like they are in bold print.

Don't be afraid to read some commentaries or listen to sermons about the Book of John. After all, Paul writes, "**Study** to shew thyself **approved** unto God, a workman that needeth not to be ashamed, rightly dividing the word of truth." (2 Timothy 2:15) (KJV)

In other words, while its admirable to read the Bible, and I strongly encourage you to do so, spend a little extra time in study with other sources. There are many worthwhile study guides available. If you don't know which one to pick, ask your pastor or church leadership. They can help you.

You may have heard some say or even said yourself, "I wish I knew God's will for my life." Everything you need to know is in the pages of His word. The beautiful thing is He is more than willing to teach you. We'll talk about hearing the voice of God later.

After you've spent time in the Book of John getting reacquainted with God's love for you, I would suggest going to the Book of Psalms. The Psalms is the "song book" or praise and worship of its day. You might ask what good it does to read those writings and the answer comes straight from...the Bible.

Psalm 22:3 tells us that God inhabits the praises of His people. The Psalms are nothing but praises to God written mostly by King David; yes, that David from "David and Goliath."

We determined above that fear can not possibly come from God. If that is true and that God inhabits the praises of His people, meaning you and me, then fear cannot stay in the room where God is being praised.

In addition, the Book of Psalms contains one of the most beautiful passages of comfort ever written. "The Lord is my shepherd" is one of the most quoted passages in history and especially poignant in times of loss and distress.

After you've worked through the Psalms, may I suggest the Proverbs (right after Psalms) that provide wisdom to a world sadly lacking in it.

By the time you've finished all that, you may be ready to spend time elsewhere in the Bible. What's more, systematic Bible study becomes habit forming and stress relieving.

The Power of Prayer

Another item our Sunday School teacher taught us besides reading our Bibles was to pray. For many of us though, our prayer life growing up consisted up blessing the evening meal, ("God is great, God is good, and we thank Him, for our food.") to our bed time prayer ("Now I lay me down to sleep...")

We never grasped the potential in prayer during those years. Later we may have used prayer in desperation ("God, if you're up there...") or in trying to make a deal with Him ("Lord, if you'll get me out of this, I promise...")

Prayer from desperation is no prayer at all. Prayers of complaint do nothing for us. It's the power behind a faith backed prayer that gets God's attention.

Previously, we discussed spiritual warfare and the powers that we wage that war against. In our earlier discussion of the grieved Father who came before Jesus asking him to cast the spirits out of his son, what we didn't talk about was that the poor father had brought his son to the disciples and asked them to cast the spirit out.

After the young man was set free, the disciples asked Jesus why they couldn't cast the spirit out of the boy. Jesus took a moment to teach them about faith and then he concluded with "However, this kind does not go out except by prayer and fasting." (Matthew 17:21 NKJV)

Jesus could not over emphasize the power that He Himself got from praying to His father. He spent His last free hours on earth in prayer working through the spiritual warfare that would end with His going to the cross.

You cannot expect to live a successful Christian life without a consistent time of prayer.

To a person who has not developed a deep walk with God, prayer can look like something that is, at best, a ritual and at worst, a complete waste of time. We may attempt to pray by using old King James language with "thee" and "thou." We may find our attention drifting to the duties of the day, or a difficult conversation we had at lunch.

Quite often, a person might not even know where to begin. God may seem like a complete stranger and the idea of prayer a totally foreign concept.

Thankfully, Jesus Himself, was, as expected, a master teacher at this subject. In Luke Chapter 11, the disciples have taken note that Jesus conversed with the Father consistently and powerfully through prayer. This observation must have created a desire within the disciples as one of the twelve said to Jesus, "Lord teach us to pray, as John also taught his disciples." (Luke 11:1)

Jesus, understanding that He was not only teaching prayer to His disciples but to those of us who would follow him for generations, gave a model prayer that we recite to this day:

^{9} After this manner therefore pray ye: Our Father which art in heaven, Hallowed be thy name.
^{10} Thy kingdom come, Thy will be done in earth, as it is in heaven.
^{11} Give us this day our daily bread.
^{12} And forgive us our debts, as we forgive our debtors.
^{13} And lead us not into temptation, but deliver us from evil: For thine is the kingdom, and the power, and the glory, forever. Amen.

While it is wonderful to pray this prayer and even comforting at times, Jesus was actually presenting this as a model or guideline for prayer. He wasn't wanting us to pray this as part of our routine, but to use it to develop our own conversation with God that would result in a life altering relationship.

Notice in verse 9, Jesus starts, "After this manner therefore pray ye:" In other words, "here are the components that should go into your conversation with the Father.

"Our Father which art in heaven…"

If you look through the writings that span His ministry, Jesus began many of His statements with, "My Father." Here, Jesus says that His heavenly Father is ours too. For some religions, the concept of God is a demanding and punishing entity who appears to be angry all the time. Unfortunately, many of us believe that about God.

Yet Jesus describes this relationship as one of a dad relating to his child. He is reminding us that this time of prayer is not only important to us but it is very important to God. He loves to have conversations with us and does participate in our prayers.

How important are your prayers to God? "And when he had taken it, the four living creatures and the twenty-four elders fell down before the Lamb. Each one had a harp and they were holding golden bowls full of incense, which are the prayers of God's people." (Revelation 5:8, NIV)

That's how important your prayers are to God. They are so important that they are as sweet as the fragrant smell of incense before Him." You may think today you don't matter to God, that He doesn't even remember your name. That's what the liar wants you to believe. But, the truth is that God is so hungry to hear from you that when you do pray it is precious to Him as it comes before His throne.

"Hallowed be Thy name."

As precious as your prayers are to Him, God wants to be just as precious to you. Hallowed simply means holy or set apart. It is a signal of worship before the Creator of Heaven and Earth.

Think of it this way. In ages past, one did not enter into a King's chambers, stroll up to the throne, wrap an arm around the King's shoulder and say, "Hey King, how ya doin' today?"

In most throne rooms, visitors were required to bow once upon entering the room, proceed a few feet, bow again, and repeat until arriving at a respectful distance from the condescension of royalty. The royal subject was not allowed to make eye contact with the sovereign, must get to the point, state their business, and then silently wait on the King's pleasure. Then the entire process was repeated on the way back out the door; always facing the king, never looking up until finally exiting the throne room.

While we are not required to go to such lengths as we approach the throne of God, we still should enter our time with Him respectfully, acknowledging the Holiness of His name, and the fact that He is Lord of all.

Very rarely do the books of Chronicles come into play for instruction for the Christian. However, in 2 Chronicles 20 Jehoshaphat was leading Judah against the forces of the Moabites and the Ammonites. He proclaimed a fast throughout Judah and lead his people in prayer to God asking for His deliverance.

God then spoke to His people telling them they would not have to fight but that He would, indeed, deliver them. Notice verse 22, "The moment they began their shouts and praises, the LORD set an ambush against the Ammonites, Moabites, and the inhabitants of Mount Seir who came to fight against Judah, and they were defeated." (Christian Standard Bible)

God can and will create an ambush for the enemy the moment we begin to praise Him. Why? He inhabits our praises. He lives in them. Satan wants no part of that.

"Thy kingdom come, Thy will be done on earth, as it is in heaven"

Here, we acknowledge that we desire for God's will, mercy and love reign throughout the earth as it clearly does in heaven. In addition, it is our commitment to God to do our part in spreading the message of God throughout the earth.

"Give us this day, our daily bread"

Part of our prayer should be a recognition of God's gracious blessings to us every day. We simply tell God how grateful we are that He has provided our every need. We are also declaring that He is more than enough to see us through the day.

 Remember in our discussion of fear, we noted that part of fear is doubting that God is enough to see us through our difficulties. Give us this day, our daily bread is a strong statement of confidence in a God that is more than enough to meet our needs physically, spiritually, emotionally and mentally.

"...and forgive us our debts, as we forgive our debtors."

Approaching the throne of God, it is imperative that we do with a heart steeped in forgiveness. Hebrews 4:16 tells us we should "...therefore come boldly unto the throne of grace, that we may obtain mercy, and find grace to help in the time of need." (KJV)

There are few things as bad as trying to pray to God with that feeling of guilt that not all is right in our lives. God offers us forgiveness but also requires forgiveness from us. An unforgiving heart is one that usually lives in deception, blaming others for the things we have been a part of.

"...and lead us not into temptation..."

You might think this is a very interesting thing for Jesus to include in a model prayer. How would God lead us into temptation? Here we are asking God to supervise our daily lives and help guide us away from the temptations that this world holds for us. It reflects our wish to avoid the dangers of sin and evil. It also acknowledges God's ability to keep us from the control of the enemy.

"…but deliver us from evil."

Here we are asking God's divine assistance in resisting the advances of the Evil one. James 4:7 instructs us to "Resist the devil and he will flee from you." While common sense tells us to avoid situations that bring us face to face with evil, we ask for God's help to not be placed in situations that are out of our control.

When Jesus was facing his last hours, He turned to prayer to strengthen Himself for the ordeal he was about to face. Yet in this dire time, His burden was for you.

In John 17:15 He prays, "I pray not that thou shouldest take them out of the world, but that thou shouldest keep them from evil." In verse 20 He goes on to pray, "Neither I pray for these alone, but for them also which shall believe on me through their word."

In verse 15 Jesus makes it clear that He is praying for your protection from the Evil one and then He is praying directly for you in verse 20! It is important for each believer to pray for protection from the enemy every day.

"For Thine is the Kingdom, and the Power, and the Glory Forever, Amen."

In ending the model prayer, Jesus instructs us to circle back to praise and recognition of the Glory of God. He alone has the ability to support an everlasting Kingdom. He alone has the power to withstand any circumstances that may be invented by the enemy. Therefore, He alone is worthy of Glory. Amen.

You might say, "Are you sure God is expecting me to say all that just to pray to Him?" Of course not. Jesus was very clear when He gave these instructions, "After this manner, therefore, pray ye." God simply wants us to talk to Him.

Prayer is a resource for us not only in times of trouble, but as a proactive and protective assault against the strongholds of the enemy. Furthermore, combined with consistent Bible study, its where we get direction for our lives, it's the source of wisdom, knowledge, peace and strength.

I come from a long line of praying people. My great-grandfather, according to my Dad, would quietly steal away from the farm in Tennessee and find a place in the gulley, get to his knees and pray like he thought God was deaf. He prayed for everyone in his family including a red-headed little boy (my dad) who was watching from a distance and thought he hadn't been noticed.

I recall my late mother stretched face down across her bed praying out loud in the Spirit, my dad, a pastor for over 56 years, walking the floor of the church while no one was there, praying for everyone that came to his mind.

With that in mind, my prayer closet is my car. Yours can be wherever you find a quiet place to be alone with Him.

My usual prayer is along these lines:

"Dear Heavenly Father, I come before you today first thanking you for who you are. You are the creator of heaven and earth, the Mighty God, the Prince of Peace, the Everlasting Father, and you still want to talk to me. I stand amazed that You want to have a conversation with me."

"I thank you for the breath of life you give me each day, for the ability to think, and to love and to enjoy the gifts you've given me."

"Father, if I have offended you or come short of your expectations in any way, please forgive me. I am more than happy to forgive and ask for forgiveness where others are concerned."

"In John 17 you prayed for our protection against the evil one. I ask you today to please protect me and those I love against him. In your name I rebuke the devourer and resist any of his temptations."

After these things, I just talk to Him about the things that are on my mind. Believe it or not, if they concern me, they concern Him. People sometimes believe that God is too busy to be bothered by their little problems when, in fact, just the opposite is true. God is so concerned with us that He sent Jesus to die for us.

Let me encourage you to at least begin a prayer life. You will find it is habit forming. You'll soon feel that something is missing from your day if you can't spend time with God.

Now, one last thought on prayer. Nobody likes a conversation that is one sided and nothing is worse than to be with someone who only wants to talk and has no desire to hear what we have to say. God is not just somebody, but, He still would like to talk to you.

Take some time after your prayer to get quiet.

"Be still and know that I am God" (Psalm 46:10)

"The Lord will fight for you. You need only to be still." (Exodus 14:14)

"Be still before the Lord and wait patiently for Him…" (Psalm 37:7)

"For God alone, O my soul, wait in silence, for my hope is from Him." (Psalm 62:5)

God will certainly speak to you. Don't look for an audible voice because He usually speaks to our mind. Yet, His voice is unmistakable. Don't look for an audible voice, but then again, after all, He is God and can speak to us however He wishes.

Finally, believe that God loves to answer prayer. He absolutely delights in it. Jesus said, "You have not because you ask not. And, "…I will do whatever you ask in my name, so that the Father may be glorified in the Son." (John 14:13, NIV)

Preach Yourself a Sermon

Since 1988 I've preached and taught many, many times and it always amazes me how God reveals things or opens up scripture in ways I hadn't even considered when I was preparing to speak. Does God only speak to Pastors and Evangelists? That would be like saying that God only inhabits the praises of a worship leader or soloist.

If you don't think God will actually speak to you, let me challenge you to try this experiment: Preach yourself a sermon. I don't mean just lecture yourself on a topic, but actually identify a piece of scripture that you find applicable to your life. Then prepare a sermon. You might say, "you've got to be kidding." You have no idea how many times God speaks during a sermon.

Find a quiet place, sit down with your Bible, your study materials and a note pad or your computer.

Step 1 – Go ahead and give it a title. For instance: "God's Mercy is New Every Morning," just to pick a topic.

Step 2 – Find your text. In this case, let's choose Lamentations 3:22-23: The steadfast love of the LORD never ceases. His mercies never come to an end; they are new every morning; great is your faithfulness. (English Standard Version)

Step 4 – Get an opening just for you. Example: "Good morning, self. I want to talk to you this morning from the book of Lamentations. I believe God has great encouragement in store for you today, so open your Bible and turn to Lamentations 3:22-23 and let's dig in."

Step 3 – Iron out three points with a couple of subpoints for each. After each point or subpoint, try to expound a little further past the outline by applying that subpoint to something going on in your life.

Let's try it:

1. The promises of God never fail
    a. Therefore, this verse applies to me and anyone else who needs it
    b. I can rely on Him to be consistent, steadfast
    c. His Word is forever, it will not cease
2. His steadfast love
    a. Was demonstrated through the sacrifice of Jesus
    b. Was meant for "Whosoever"
    c. His love is there through any circumstance
3. His mercies never come to an end
    a. I have His promise that my sins and fear are wiped away every day
    b. He has no remembrance of my short comings
    c. His faithfulness is beyond great, it is my lifeline

Step 5 – Closing. Every good sermon needs a closing. Let's apply this to our lives. "So, in closing, my dear self, God wants you to know that fear has no place in your life. He wants you to know that His mercy, His love, and His faithfulness were gifts He presented from the cross as if you were the only one who ever needed them. Now, my dear self, let's pray together and release our fear and anxiety to Him because He is more than willing to take it all away."

Again, you might think, "If my family ever got wind of this they would have me committed." Really, this is no different than preparing any other Bible study. The challenge I have for you is to pay close attention as you talk to yourself and what really does come into your mind. The Holy Spirit is our Teacher and Guide and you will be amazed at how He teaches through scripture. The word of God is alive and the pages will begin to jump out at you.

If you still think this is a little crazy, consider these scriptures:

*"This Book of the Law **shall not depart from your mouth**, but you shall meditate in it day and night, that you may observe to do according to all that is written in it. For then you will make your way prosperous, and then you will have good success." (Joshua 1:8, NKJV)*

*"Let the words of my mouth and the meditation of my heart be acceptable in your sight, O L*ORD*, my rock and my redeemer. (Psalm 19:14, ESV)*

"So shall my word be that goes out from my mouth; it shall not return to me empty, but it shall accomplish that which I purpose, and shall succeed in the thing for which I sent it. (Isaiah 55:11, ESV)

Oh, one more thing…don't forget to take up an offering! (Just kidding)

The Power of Giving

One of the biggest misconceptions is that God needs our money. From one side of our mouths we say "He owns the cattle on a thousand hills." Then, from the other side we mumble, "The church is always after my money."

Understanding that money can be a very touchy subject for most of us, the first concept we need to grasp is "The earth is the Lord's, and the fulness thereof; the world and they that dwell within it." (Psalm 24:1) In other words, once we get rid of the idea of ownership giving is much easier to understand. Everything is God's.

You might say, "I go in to work everyday and earn my paycheck. How is that God's?"

Deuteronomy 8:17-18 is very clear: "You might say in your heart, "The power and strength of my hands have made this wealth for me. But remember that it is the Lord your God who gives you the power to gain wealth…"

The Bible speaks in plain terms as well about what is due God.

Malachi Chapter 3:

[8] Will a man rob God? Yet ye have robbed me. But ye say, Wherein have we robbed thee? In tithes and offerings.

[9] Ye are cursed with a curse: for ye have robbed me, even this whole nation.

[10] Bring ye all the tithes into the storehouse, that there may be meat in mine house, and prove me now herewith, saith the LORD of hosts, if I will not open you the windows of heaven, and pour you out a blessing, that there shall not be room enough to receive it.

[11] And I will rebuke the devourer for your sakes, and he shall not destroy the fruits of your ground; neither shall your vine cast her fruit before the time in the field, saith the LORD of hosts.

Having read each of the scriptures here are a few things we really need to grasp:

- God owns it all and we are merely stewarding what He has placed in our hands
- He expects the first tenth to be returned to Him. That is our tithe and is not a free will offering
- He considers those who do not return the first tenth to be robbers.
- If we follow His plan of giving He will rebuke the devourer for our sake.
- Anything we offer above that first tenth is out of our love for Him and our concern for others.

The First Tenth

You may have heard the term "tithe" before and usually in regard to giving. You may also have looked at your own finances and thought, "there is no way I can afford to give God ten percent of my income. I can barely make ends meet as it is."

Realize that severe financial crises are another source of fear. Fear that we may lose the things we have. Fear that we will never be able to afford the things we want. Fear that financial collapse may damage or even end a marriage or relationship with our families.

The concept of tithing was put in place even before the days of Abraham. In the Book of Genesis, Abraham was given victory over the King of Elam. He recovered all the enemy had stolen including family and livestock. Upon his return, Abraham was met by the King of Salem, Melchizedek, who met him with wine and bread. After Melchizedek blessed him, Abraham gave him one tenth of all the goods he had captured.

In various scriptures, God instructs the Children of Israel that the first tenth was holy to Him; including the first born of cattle and the first fruit of any of their increase.

For us today, God has not changed in His attitude toward the first-fruit. As we read in Malachi 3:8 when He asked if Israel would rob Him in tithes and offerings. He judged Israel immediately in 3:9 when he stated, "Ye are cursed with a curse, even this whole nation..."

So, how can we honor God with our first fruit? God expects the first tenth to be returned to Him as an acknowledgement that He is the giver of life and all we receive to maintain life. Here are a few considerations that may help where tithing is concerned:

- On payday or when you work through your bills, the first payment is always your tithe.
- It should be on your gross pay. You may think you should only pay on your net but, in fact, your payroll taxes are actually another bill you would have to pay if your employer did not withhold.
- If you are self-employed, be consistent with your giving period, but, whenever you get income, set aside the first tenth for God.

Here is the challenge for you. When you think you can't afford to give God His tithe, do it anyway and remind Him of His word concerning giving in verse 10:

"and prove me now herewith, saith the LORD of hosts, if I will not open you the windows of heaven, and pour you out a blessing, that there shall not be room enough to receive it." (Malachi 3:10)

At that moment, or that paycheck, when you feel you can least afford to pay your tithe, mark your budget, take note of your bank balance, then turn it over to God and wait to see if He honors all He promises. He will pour out His blessings. One of the ways He may bless is that your belongings may last longer or need fewer repairs. You might be blessed with a bonus, extra hours or some other means, but you will know without a doubt that the blessing has come from God and God alone.

As God blesses in response to our return of His tithe, your anxiety over money will lessen. Your dependence upon Him will soar and your fear where His provision is concerned will ebb away.

Tithes vs. Offerings

Aren't tithes and offerings the same thing? As seem in Malachi Chapter 3, God separates them when He says, "...wherein have we robbed Thee, in tithes and offerings." Again, tithes are ten percent or the first-fruit of our income. That part belongs to God and we are simply returning something that is already His.

Offerings are above and beyond. Tithe is a matter of obedience. 1 Samuel Chapter 15 tells us, "...Behold, to obey is better than sacrifice." Tithe is our obedience, offerings are our sacrifice. Sacrifice speaks to the condition of the heart. It is about compassion, about a loving heart, about a grateful spirit.

While God has already spoken all He has to say about your tithe, the offering is the fertile ground where He can grow you into a generous giver who loves people and loves the Kingdom of God. It could be an opportunity to support a missionary in a far away land. It could be coming to the aid of the homeless or poor in your home town. It could be giving your time as well as your treasure to someone as a witness of the Love of God for them. Offering is where He can challenge us, stretch us and speak to us. The area of offering is where we can hear the voice of God and come away with a joyous heart where no spirit of fear would dare approach.

Love

*"For God hath not given us the Spirit of Fear, but of Power, **and of Love**, and of a sound mind."*

Christ's Love for Us

I think anyone would agree that our world today is scarred and wounded. Love seems to be in short supply and highly treasured. Marriages suffer, children are wounded and bruised, our cultures clash, countries around the world compete sometimes to the point of violence for what resources are available.

We sing about love, write poems, and churn out movies and plays about what our idea of love should be. We long for it, reach for it and too often are disappointed by it.

The fact is, we have lost sight of what perfect love really is and have traded it for more lies of the enemy.

I was told once that the one thing a woman wants in her life is unconditional love. In other words, she wants a love that she can depend upon "for better or worse, for richer or poorer." The sad truth in many cases is that love does seem to be conditional for us. Many value external beauty and as it fades so does love. Often, we base love on the other person's bank account and when that starts to dwindle pressure comes on the relationship and is not always survived.

As a result, fear shows its ugly head and contributes to the destruction of our marriages and relationships with family members. In areas of blended families or people who have been married multiple times, fear is a result of past hurt as we start to expect a repetition of the same behaviors and results as before.

What we really want and value more than money, more than luxuries and more than even youth is a perfect love. We watch a couple on their wedding day and can see it in their eyes; they are expecting a perfect marriage and perfect love.

How do we find that perfect love?

What would you think if you found a person who only had eyes for you? Someone who only cared about what troubles you, had your best interest at heart and was so in love with you that they would push you out of harm's way and take injury upon themselves in your place.

What if you met someone who, just at the worst possible time in your life, took the blame for everything you did wrong, never asking anything in return? If you had someone like that as your own, fear and anxiety would never enter into the relationship

1 John 4:18 tells us that "There is no fear in love; but perfect love casteth out fear." Did you see that word again? Fear. Part of our original equation is that love overrides fear every time. Even more important God's love is unconditional. And greater still, in this verse we see that perfect love doesn't just make fear less of a problem in our lives, John writes that perfect love "casts out" fear. To cast something away is to throw it, boot it, punt it, send it with great force. Fear has to go in the face of perfect love; and go quickly.

We all know the story of Jesus' torture, death and resurrection. The most amazing part of the story is that He died for us knowing He was dying for abject sinners. There is no scenario that sees us deserve this love.

Each New Year I write a message to my two children and their spouses. It is my desire that they see a model, not of a perfect Father, but a Father that tries to represent in a small way God's love for them. One particular New Year I told them that my prayer for them that year was that God would reveal just how fascinated and enamored He was of them.

How do I know He is fascinated and enamored of them? Because I am. Nothing has changed since my children were born. I was fascinated with them then, and now, even though they are adults, the room seems to brighten when they walk in. Everything they do and say is of great interest to me.

Jesus said in Matthew 7:11, "If you, then, though you are evil, know how to give good gifts to your children, how much more will your Father in heaven give good gifts to those who ask him!" That's how I can tell my children that God is fascinated with them.

God looks at each of us the same way. He created you and is riveted by you, so much so that, "...while we were yet sinners, Christ died for us." (Romans 5:8)

An Overflowing Love

There is an old rule that says if a young child is quiet for very long something is wrong. I can remember my sister disappearing at my grandmother's house wen we were young. After some time, my mother came looking for her only to find my grandmother's bathroom newly decorated in a coat of talcum powder. It was an overflowing mess.

Overflowing can either be good or bad according to your point of view. When pouring a carbonated drink we try to estimate at what point the expanding carbonation will overflow the glass. Should the drink creep over the sides, there is a mess to clean up.

However, take a five-year-old to get an ice cream sundae and when the chocolate syrup, sprinkles and whipped cream start to overflow the container, yes, it may be a mess but to that child it is the most glorious spill they've ever seen.

Earlier when we discussed tithes and offerings we noted Malachi 3:10, "and prove me now herewith, saith the LORD of hosts, if I will not open you the windows of heaven, and pour you out a blessing, that there shall not be room enough to receive it." Since God can never change and is consistent in all of his dealings, it stands to reason that His love would be an overflowing fountain pouring out upon us as well.

As we experience the purest love we have ever known, it makes sense that our hearts would begin to overflow with His love. Where we've need forgiveness, he forgives. Where we need financial blessings, he pours out beyond all we could ever expect. And where we need mercy, His mercy is "...new every morning."

The beauty of overflowing love is the wonderful mess it makes. Overflowing love just oozes out of our hearts. Jesus had something to say about overflowing love: "A good man brings good things out of the good stored up in his heart, and an evil man brings evil things out of the evil stored up in his heart. For the mouth speaks what the heart is full of." (Luke 6:45 NIV)

Further, Matthew 6:21 states, "for where your treasure is, there will your heart be also." (KV) Normally this passage is associated with financial giving, but perhaps Jesus was talking about something more than just our offerings here. If you look at these two verses together, "For the mouth speaks what the heart is full of," and "for where your treasure is, there will your heart be also," you can see that His love for us, as our greatest treasure, overflows in our heart and comes out of our mouths.

Again, "there is no fear in the perfect love of God." That love is our treasure, it overflows from our hearts into our mouths and does away with fear as we speak our faith. The love of God in our lives completely transforms us from a person living in fear to a dynamic person who knows themselves to be the most loved and most loving person on earth.

That overflowing then coats our daily relationships. It coats our marriage, our kids, our in-laws and even those crusty neighbors that live next door. Does it happen overnight? It can. After all, we can never limit God. But if it takes a while that's ok too.

Overflowing love coming from our mouths may not be easy at times. Some of us enjoy just saying what we think. Others of us cope with difficulties with humor or sarcasm. Many of us let our anger come out in our conversations often hurting the ones close to us. We do need to realize that past hurt caused by the things we say may be difficult for others to forgive and overcome. Give it time.

In the meanwhile, there are a couple of ways we can pray that might help speed up the situation.

- "Set a guard over my mouth, O Lord, keep watch over the door of my lips." (Psalm 141:3, NIV)
- "Hide your face from my sins and blot out all my iniquity. Create in me a pure heart, O God, and renew a steadfast spirit within me." (Psalm 51:10, NIV)

In both cases, King David was crying out to God. In Psalm 141, David is asking for God to keep him away from wickedness. In the 51st Psalm He is repenting. These two scriptures have become a part of my everyday prayer and to my amazement, I find that I really don't need to speak about everything that passes by me. I really do need God to continually put a watch over my mouth and always renew a steadfast spirit in me.

I wish I could tell you after all these years that I am perfect in each of these two areas but I fail spectacularly at times. However, I know that I can feel a change in my heart and that as I spend more time in prayer and praise, love is much closer to my lips than sarcasm and criticism.

Matthew 5:37 councils us to "Let your communication be yea, yea, nay, nay, for whatever is more than these cometh of evil." (KJV) In other words, we are accountable for every word that comes out of ours mouths including the damage that we do with them. Furthermore, James 3:6 uses these strong terms, "The tongue also is a fire, a world of evil among the parts of the body. It corrupts the whole body, sets the whole course of one's life on fire, and is itself set on fire by hell." (NIV)

Sometimes our relationships can self-destruct simply from a lack of constraint. We feel we can change the paths of the people in our lives by our words. We may disapprove of something someone close to us is doing and the expectation of our criticism is 1) that they will amend their ways to our approved idea of what they should do and 2) get it "off my chest" making us feel better.

In fact, what usually happens is the other party digs their heels in either in rebellion or spite resulting in you not only not feeling better, but actually feeling angrier than you did. What is worse is the cycle just continues until at some point the relationship is irrevocably broken.

Overflowing Love: Husbands and Wives

One of the most challenging relationships for any of us is with our spouses. We love them, but they can be the very person who can get on our last nerve, push our button, and drive us insane all at the same time.

Arguably the most controversial passages of scripture can be found in Ephesians, Chapter 5:

[22] Wives, submit yourselves unto your own husbands, as unto the Lord.
[23] For the husband is the head of the wife, even as Christ is the head of the church: and he is the savior of the body.
[24] Therefore as the church is subject unto Christ, so let the wives be to their own husbands in ever thing.
[25] Husbands, love your wives, even as Christ also loved the church, and gave himself for it;
[26] That he might sanctify and cleanse it with the washing of water by the word,

*²⁷ That he might present it to himself a glorious church, not having spot, or wrinkle, or any such thing; but that it should be holy and without blemish.
²⁸ So ought men to love their wives as their own bodies. He that loveth his wife loveth himself.*

So many couples have misconstrued these verses letting the words dissolve into arguments. The wife wants nothing to do with such an old-fashioned concept as submitting to a husband. But, if we dig deeper, we can come to a different understanding.

One of the deepest sources of fear is the mistrust of the other person in our marriage. In a world that devalues marriage on a nearly daily basis, the courts are full of couples who have gone from trust to simply throwing away their lives together.

Look at verse 23 just a little closer. "For the husband is the head of the wife, even as Christ is the head of the church: and he is the savior of the body." That comparison can be daunting upon closer review. Christ gave His very life for His bride, the church, meaning us. The husband is to be willing to put only Christ Himself above the needs of his wife. Not the kids, not the job, not golf, nothing.

Ladies, if you were married to someone who had only your deepest concerns at heart, who cared enough about you to die for you, wouldn't that be someone you would gladly submit to? As we said above, that word, "submit" is the sticking point; and not just for women. Our society today cares mostly about self. We spend more time worrying about our rights, about our opinions and about our point of view that listening and caring for others.

Wouldn't we have a great world if we submitted to each other the way Jesus submitted to His Father's will?

A Sound Mind

*"For God hath not given us the Spirit of Fear, but of Power, and of Love, **and of a Sound Mind.**"*

Difficult Times

During June of 2020, the Centers for Disease Control (CDC) stated that 40% of U.S. adults struggled with mental health or substance use. 31% reported anxiety and depression symptoms and 11% seriously considered suicide.

During the best of times life has become challenging for so many of us. If we add quarantine, job loss, death of loved ones and unprecedented uncertainty, the long-term effects upon our senses of well-being is staggering.

In generations past, those who suffered from mental illness were regarded as unstable to the point of being unreliable and unemployable. Today, we prescribe, counsel, and treat as much as we can but, at times, the battle seems to be out of control.

Many Christians today report an overwhelming fear and unfortunately in many cases they are unable or ill-equipped to fight back against the enemy. While this book does not intend to offer "cures" we do want to discuss some areas we may be able to help ourselves.

First, in some cases, anxiety and depression turns out to be a spiritual issue. Think about the conflicting messages our mind and spirit take in every day. God's word tells us how to live according to His commands, not so He can control us, but that in His infinite wisdom He can help us head off disaster in our lives.

When we turn on the television, go to a movie or listen to the radio in most cases the communication is contrary to what God tells us. Situation comedies seem to treat lying and deceit as harmless pranks that are meant to be humorous. Many movies extol cheating on a spouse or visiting violence on an unsuspecting neighbor. Contrary to today's values, music tells us it's just fine to have sex with anyone we meet but it rarely discusses the results that may include broken families, unwanted pregnancies that lead to abortion, or substance abuse that may result in depression or even death.

When brought to account for such excesses, our culture, in a weak response, says traditional values are "old fashioned," "out of touch," or unabashedly ridicule Christian culture as unenlightened.

What we allow into our lives can confuse God's message to us. The value we may put on the entertainment industry, the opinions of sports stars and actors, or even our government officials most often is in direct conflict with the word of God. It is the "Big Lie."

When we allow lies to cloud our view of reality, we actually open the door for the enemy to have influence over us. Let me remind you that the Bible branded Satan as a murderer and the father of lies. There is no truth in him.

What is worse is when we live a life of fantasy, whether it be pornography or even the old soap operas, over time our world view is changed and that world we've been experiencing starts to be our reality. Is it any wonder that many leading citizens as well as every day people are caught doing illegal and immoral activities that wreck lives and shatter futures? We've come to believe that truth is subjective and reality is whatever we make it.

We also established that in Genesis 1:1, God's Spirit hovered over the deep. The Holy Spirit was one of the very first subjects mentioned in the Bible. The spirit realm is real and as we leave the door open it will be spirits of another kind that can take up residence. This is not to necessarily indicate that you are demon possessed, but instead spirits that are contrary to the word of God may have influence.

Opening the Door to the Holy Spirit

There will come a time when we finally realize that we have been deceived. We have believed the lie. We have allowed to enemy to tell us, "God is ok with the way you're living. He understands that you've had it hard and He is fine with you." We rationalize sin and deceive ourselves.

You might think, "If God knows the problem I'm having here, why doesn't He just do something?" The facts are:

      1) He will not be around sin.
      2) He will not come without being invited
      3) He will come if asked and
      4) His Holy Spirit will continue to work with you in a still, small voice.

Trust me when I tell you that "mind over matter" will not help in this case. This is a spiritual battle. We sing the song, "Holy Spirit, You are welcome here." It's a wonderful song with a wonderful message but for me it is more "Holy Spirit, you are desperately needed, desired, required and longed for." The Holy Spirit of God is whom Jesus described as "the comforter" who will lead us into all truth. The very first truth He will lead us in is that we are hopeless without God.

How do we open the door to the Holy Spirit? Simply ask. We go back to the subject of prayer and simply ask Him (not it) to make His home within us. Jesus explained it like this:

"I will ask the Father, and he will give you another helper who will be with you forever. [17] That helper is the Spirit of Truth. The world cannot accept him, because it doesn't see or know him. You know him, because he lives with you and will be in you." (John 14:16-17 God's Word Translation)

Jesus was very concerned about His relationship with the Father and had much to say about the subject.

Therefore, Jesus answered and was saying to them, "Truly, truly, I say to you, the Son can do nothing of Himself, unless it is something He sees the Father doing; for whatever the Father does, these things the Son also does in like manner. (John 5:19)

"I and the Father are one." (John 10:30)

"For I have come down from heaven, not to do My own will, but the will of Him who sent Me. This is the will of Him who sent Me, that of all that He has given Me I lose nothing, but raise it up on the last day." (John 6:38-39)

The wonderful thing about His relationship with the Father was that he provided the same relationship to God for us through His death and resurrection. You are related to God Himself through Christ.

The Value of Quiet

The world is a noisy place and seems to demand that we listen to it. We are bombarded with a wave of sound like no other generation before. I recall the first time I spent the night in New York City back in the 1970's I was astounded by the wall of noise coming up from the streets all night. From beeping car horns, to sirens, to people yelling at each other, it really did seem to be the city that doesn't sleep.

The Bible instructs us on several occasions to find a place of quiet and solitude to be with the Father, Psalm 46:10 tells us to "Be still and know that I am God." Psalm 62:1 says "For God alone my soul waits in silence; from him comes my salvation."

Did you know that God loves to talk to His children? Today, we look at people a little funny when they say they hear from God, but the fact is, He really loves it. You might think, in your busy world, you have no time to get quiet before God but it is surprising just how much time you can make for Him.

He tells us in His word to "Pray without ceasing." (1 Thessalonians 5:17) That doesn't mean to walk around all day with your eyes closed saying "amen" every 15 minutes. What it does refer to is a condition of the heart where our minds are always open to Him in an attitude of conversation.

As mentioned before, I have found my early morning drive to work to be a perfect time to pray, but even more important, to get quiet and just listen. Many times, I will have thoughts or something will come into my mind; an answer to a problem, a piece of wisdom, that I hadn't considered before. I know perfectly well that the Holy Spirit is present.

I like to take my showers in the evening and as soon as I step in that's my time to simply praise Him and even sing a song of worship. Nothing like singing in the shower. It is so very important to keep those channels of communication open with Him and feel the strength that comes from just being in His presence.

Fear vs. Sleep

One area that I've had trouble with for many years is the ability to sleep. It seems so simple. You close your eyes and off you go. It is not always that simple. Sometimes our inability to sleep may be physiological in nature but for many of us, the cares of life crowd in and rob us of our rest.

The enemy loves to operate late at night. Many years ago, the Lord gave me a special concern for the mental and spiritual battles that go on when we should be sleeping. For those facing life threatening disease, Satan has a field day filling them with fear and anxiety until sleep is pure fantasy. He fills their nights with lies layered upon lies robbing them of not just sleep but of the very joy of living.

Those who are in the middle of a job crisis, marital issues, or financial burdens find themselves flipping through the channels of late-night television just praying for morning to come.   Aging comes in to play as older adults might be able to fall asleep but find it a challenge to stay asleep waking in the wee hours of the morning.

How do we cope with the loss of sleep and the accompanying fatigue of getting through each day?

The Lord begin to show me how to deal with this only recently when I brought it up to Him. He instructed me that He wanted me to very quickly recap the highlights and even low lights of the day, but then immediately move on from it.

He wanted me to begin to ask the Holy Spirit to fill me up to overflowing. He wanted me to welcome the Spirit into my sleep. Finally, He wanted me to confess that I wanted nothing more than to be as close to Him as I could possibly get. Instead of allowing the problems of that day to occupy my mind, I was busy worshipping and even singing in my mind. Every time I awakened in the night I would go right back to this chorus:

Holy Spirit, Breathe on Me
Holy Spirit, Let me see
All the things you are

All the things you want me to be
Holy Spirit, Breathe on Me

Wayne Drain, a Pastor from Arkansas, recently shared a song the Lord had given Him about sleep. He describes an encounter with the Lord where he explained that he was only sleeping three to five hours a night. The Lord simply said to him, "Be quiet." Pastor Drain went on to say that Lord began to sing over him starting with the words, "Go to sleep my child I love you."

Perhaps you might think the Lord singing over you is a little far fetched but, in fact, it is scriptural. Zephaniah 3:17 says, "He will rejoice over you with gladness; He will quiet you with His love; He will rejoice over you with singing."

I will put a reference in the back of this book to let you know where you can find Pastor Drain's video on YouTube. I've shared it with friends who were struggling to sleep in the midst of crisis.

Just remember that you are loved by God, fear has no place in the perfect love of God and that Psalm 127:2 tells us, "...He giveth His beloved sleep." It is a promise and it is yours.

It's Just a Beginning

Like any other obstacle or battle we fight in life, it is very difficult to overcome fear on our own. Many times, we wonder if we can every conquer it or even how to start. I come from a line of world class, blue ribbon, championship caliber worriers. My family in past generations won awards in competitive hand-wringing, made the Super Bowl of floor-walking, and were selected to the Hall of Fame of Anxious Clock Watchers.

Seriously, we sometimes repeat what has been modeled for us and the only way we can break the cycle of fear is to rely on God. Getting release from the bondage of fear is no different than trying to break free of substance abuse.

We turn to self-help, relaxation exercises, or even long vacations yet when circumstances bring uncertainty into our lives, fear returns with a vengeance and it can be devastating. God is the only key to conquering fear.

While there is no clear-cut diagram to destroying fear in our lives, we do know He has promised to never leave us or forsake us. He will always be there for us.

Please know that you are not alone in your fight against fear. We all go through times when we may feel anxious about the world around us or our own circumstances. 'Yes, your situation may be something I've never faced or so severe that you feel your life is not worth living.

God loves you. Find time to pray. Tell God all about it including the things you wouldn't admit to anyone else. Find a body of believers. Seek Godly counsel. Take it one day at a time.

"For God hath not given us the spirit of fear; but of power, and of love, and of a sound mind."

Appendix 1

Just for Starters

- Pray
  - Don't set a time limit on prayer.
  - Don't try to pray for an hour.
  - It's not about rules.
  - He just wants to spend time with you.
- Let God Have a Turn to Talk
  - Try to find a quiet place
  - Get quiet
  - Listen for a still, small voice
- Make Sure You're in Church
  - Engage in Worship
  - Tune out distractions
  - Start a systematic tithing program
- Read the Bible
  - Start with the Book of John to learn more about God's love
  - Find a translation you understand
  - Memorize scriptures that make a difference to you
  - Enjoy video teaching each day if you can (Your church can suggest some)
  - Use study materials (Your church can suggest some)
  - Preach yourself a sermon
- Share Your Faith
  - Don't be afraid to speak to others about Christ
  - Find a prayer/accountability partner when you become fearful

Appendix 2

Quick Reference of Scriptures used in this Book

2 Timothy 1:7 – "For God has not given us the spirit of fear, but of power, and of a sound mind." (NKJV)

John 10:10 - *The thief comes only to steal and kill and destroy; I have come that they may have life, and have it to the full.*

2 Timothy 1:5 - I am reminded of your sincere faith, which first lived in your grandmother Lois and in your mother Eunice and, I am persuaded, now lives in you also.

2 Timothy 1:12 - "For this reason I also suffer these things; nevertheless, I am not ashamed, for I know whom I have believed and am persuaded that He is able to keep what I have committed to Him until that Day."

2 Timothy 3:16-17 - All Scripture *is* given by inspiration of God, and *is* profitable for doctrine, for reproof, for correction, for instruction in righteousness, that the man of God may be complete, thoroughly equipped for every good work.

Job 3:25 - For the thing which I greatly feared is come upon me.

Mark 9:14-29 - [14] When they came to the other disciples, they saw a large crowd around them and the teachers of the law arguing with them. [15] As soon as all the people saw Jesus, they were overwhelmed with wonder and ran to greet him.

[16] "What are you arguing with them about?" he asked.

[17] A man in the crowd answered, "Teacher, I brought you my son, who is possessed by a spirit that has robbed him of speech. [18] Whenever it seizes him, it throws him to the ground. He foams at the mouth, gnashes his teeth and becomes rigid. I asked your disciples to drive out the spirit, but they could not."

[19] "You unbelieving generation," Jesus replied, "how long shall I stay with you? How long shall I put up with you? Bring the boy to me."

20 So they brought him. When the spirit saw Jesus, it immediately threw the boy into a convulsion. He fell to the ground and rolled around, foaming at the mouth.

21 Jesus asked the boy's father, "How long has he been like this?"

"From childhood," he answered. **22** "It has often thrown him into fire or water to kill him. But if you can do anything, take pity on us and help us."

23 "'If you can'?" said Jesus. "Everything is possible for one who believes."

24 Immediately the boy's father exclaimed, "I do believe; help me overcome my unbelief!"

25 When Jesus saw that a crowd was running to the scene, he rebuked the impure spirit. "You deaf and mute spirit," he said, "I command you, come out of him and never enter him again."

26 The spirit shrieked, convulsed him violently and came out. The boy looked so much like a corpse that many said, "He's dead." **27** But Jesus took him by the hand and lifted him to his feet, and he stood up.

28 After Jesus had gone indoors, his disciples asked him privately, "Why couldn't we drive it out?"

29 He replied, "This kind can come out only by prayer.[a]

James 1:17 - every good and perfect gift is from above, coming down from the Father of the heavenly lights who does not change like shifting shadows

Psalm 103:12 - as far as the east is from the west so far has he removed our transgressions from us.

1 Corinthians 14:33 - God is not the author of confusion, but of peace...

Matthew 24:35 - Heaven and earth will pass away but My words, will by no means pass away

Genesis 1:1 - In the beginning God created the heaven and the earth. Now the earth was formless and empty, darkness was over the surface of the deep, and the Spirit of God was hovering over the waters

John 1:1-3 - In the beginning was the Word, and the Word was with God, and the Word was God. He was with God in the beginning. Through Him all things were made; without Him nothing was made that has been made."

Genesis 2:16-17 - And the LORD God commanded the man, "You are free to eat from any tree in the garden; but you must not eat from the tree of the knowledge of good and evil, for when you eat from it you will certainly die

John 8:44 - "…He was a murderer from the beginning, not holding the truth, for there is no truth in him. When he lies, he speaks his native language, for he is a liar and the father of lies.

Luke 10:18 - I saw Satan fall like lightning from heaven.

Galatians 5:22-23 - But the fruit of the Spirit is love, joy, peace, forbearance, kindness, goodness, faithfulness, [23] gentleness and self-control. Against such things there is no law.

2 Corinthians 10:3-5 - For though we walk in the flesh, we do not war after the flesh: (For the weapons of our warfare are not carnal, but mighty through God to the pulling down of strong holds;) Casting down imaginations, and every high thing that exalteth itself against the knowledge of God, and bringing into captivity every thought to the obedience of Christ;

Ephesians 6:12 - **For we wrestle not** against flesh and blood, but against principalities, against powers, against the rulers of the darkness of this world, against spiritual wickedness in high places

Hosea 4:6 - my people are destroyed for a lack of knowledge…

Romans 8:11 - But if the Spirit of him that raised up Jesus from the dead dwell in you, he that raised up Christ from the dead shall also quicken your mortal bodies by his Spirit that dwelleth in you.

Romans 10:17 - So faith comes by hearing, and hearing by the word of God.

Hebrews 10:25 - Not forsaking the assembling of ourselves together, as the manner of some is; but exhorting one another: and so much the more, as ye see the day approaching

John 3:16 - For God so loved the world that He gave His only begotten son, that whosoever believeth on Him should not perish but have everlasting life

2 Timothy 2:15 - Study to shew thyself **approved** unto God, a workman that needeth not to be ashamed, rightly dividing the word of truth

Psalm 22:3 - *But thou art holy, O thou that inhabitest the praises of Israel."*

Matthew 17:21 - However, this kind does not go out except by prayer and fasting

Luke 11:1 - Lord teach us to pray, as John also taught his disciples

Matthew 6:9-13 - After this manner therefore pray ye: Our Father which art in heaven, Hallowed be thy name. Thy kingdom come, Thy will be done in earth, as it is in heaven. Give us this day our daily bread. And forgive us our debts, as we forgive our debtors. And lead us not into temptation, but deliver us from evil: For thine is the kingdom, and the power, and the glory, forever. Amen.

Revelation 5:8 - And when he had taken it, the four living creatures and the twenty-four elders fell down before the Lamb. Each one had a harp and they were holding golden bowls full of incense, which are the prayers of God's people

2 Chronicles 20:22 - And when they began to sing and to praise, the LORD set ambushments against the children of Ammon, Moab, and mount Seir, which were come against Judah; and they were smitten.

Hebrews 4:16 - "…therefore come boldly unto the throne of grace, that we may obtain mercy, and find grace to help in the time of need

John 17:15-20 - I pray not that thou shouldest take them out of the world, but that thou shouldest keep them from the evil. They are not of the world, even as I am not of the world. Sanctify them through thy truth: thy word is truth. As thou hast sent me into the world, even so have I also sent them into the world. And for their sakes I sanctify myself, that they also might be sanctified through the truth. Neither pray I for these alone, but for them also which shall believe on me through their word;

Psalm 46:10 - "Be still and know that I am God"

Exodus 14:14 - "The Lord will fight for you. You need only to be still."

Psalm 37:7 - "Be still before the Lord and wait patiently for Him…"

Psalm 62:5 - "For God alone, O my soul, wait in silence, for my hope is from Him."

John 14:13 - "...I will do whatever you ask in my name, so that the Father may be glorified in the Son.

Lamentations 3:22-23 - The steadfast love of the LORD never ceases. His mercies never come to an end; they are new every morning; great is your faithfulness

Joshua 1:8 - *This Book of the Law **shall not depart from your mouth**, but you shall meditate in it day and night, that you may observe to do according to all that is written in it. For then you will make your way prosperous, and then you will have good success*

Psalm 19:14 - *Let the words of my mouth and the meditation of my heart be acceptable in your sight, O LORD, my rock and my redeemer*

Isaiah 55:11 - *So shall my word be that goes out from my mouth; it shall not return to me empty, but it shall accomplish that which I purpose, and shall succeed in the thing for which I sent it*

Psalm 24:1 - The earth is the Lord's, and the fulness thereof; the world and they that dwell within it

Deuteronomy 8:17-18 - You might say in your heart, "The power and strength of my hands have made this wealth for me. But remember that it is the Lord your God who gives you the power to gain wealth..."

Malachi 3: 8-11 - Will a man rob God? Yet ye have robbed me. But ye say, Wherein have we robbed thee? In tithes and offerings. Ye are cursed with a curse: for ye have robbed me, even this whole nation.

Bring ye all the tithes into the storehouse, that there may be meat in mine house, and prove me now herewith, saith the LORD of hosts, if I will not open you the windows of heaven, and pour you out a blessing, that there shall not be room enough to receive it.

And I will rebuke the devourer for your sakes, and he shall not destroy the fruits of your ground; neither shall your vine cast her fruit before the time in the field, saith the LORD of hosts.

1 Samuel 15:22 - Behold, to obey is better than sacrifice, and to hearken than the fat of rams.

1 John 4:18 - There is no fear in love; but perfect love casteth out fear

Matthew 7:11 - If you, then, though you are evil, know how to give good gifts to your children, how much more will your Father in heaven give good gifts to those who ask him!

Romans 5:8 - "...while we were yet sinners, Christ died for us.

Luke 6:45 - A good man brings good things out of the good stored up in his heart, and an evil man brings evil things out of the evil stored up in his heart. For the mouth speaks what the heart is full of

Matthew 6:21 - for where your treasure is, there will your heart be also."

Psalm 141:3 - Set a guard over my mouth, O Lord, keep watch over the door of my lips

Psalm 51:10 - Hide your face from my sins and blot out all my iniquity. Create in me a pure heart, O God, and renew a steadfast spirit within me

Matthew 5:37 - Let your communication be yea, yea, nay, nay, for whatever is more than these cometh of evil.

James 3:6 - The tongue also is a fire, a world of evil among the parts of the body. It corrupts the whole body, sets the whole course of one's life on fire, and is itself set on fire by hell

Ephesians 5:22-28 -

Wives, submit yourselves unto your own husbands, as unto the Lord.
23 For the husband is the head of the wife, even as Christ is the head of the church: and he is the savior of the body.
24 Therefore as the church is subject unto Christ, so let the wives be to their own husbands in ever thing.
25 Husbands, love your wives, even as Christ also loved the church, and gave himself for it;
26 That he might sanctify and cleanse it with the washing of water by the word,
27 That he might present it to himself a glorious church, not having spot, or wrinkle, or any such thing; but that it should be holy and without blemish.

[28] *So ought men to love their wives as their own bodies. He that loveth his wife loveth himself.*

John 14:16-17 - I will ask the Father, and he will give you another helper who will be with you forever. [17] That helper is the Spirit of Truth. The world cannot accept him, because it doesn't see or know him. You know him, because he lives with you and will be in you

John 5:19 - *Truly, truly, I say to you, the Son can do nothing of Himself, unless it is something He sees the Father doing; for whatever the Father does, these things the Son also does in like manner*

John 10:30 - *"I and the Father are one*

John 6:38-39 - *For I have come down from heaven, not to do My own will, but the will of Him who sent Me. This is the will of Him who sent Me, that of all that He has given Me I lose nothing, but raise it up on the last day*

Psalm 46:10 - Be still and know that I am God

Psalm 62:1 - For God alone my soul waits in silence; from him comes my salvation.

1 Thessalonians 5:17 - Pray without ceasing

Zephaniah 3:17 - He will rejoice over you with gladness; He will quiet you with His love; He will *rejoice over you with singing*

Psalm 127:2 - "...He giveth His beloved sleep

Appendix 3

Other References

Holy Spirit, Breathe on Me

Holy Spirit, Breathe on Me
Holy Spirit, Let me see
All the things you are
All the things you want me to be
Holy Spirit, Breathe on Me

Holy Spirit, Breathe On Me · The ZOE Group

A Consuming Fire ℗ 2002 Christian Music Resources, Inc.

While You are Sleeping – Wayne Drain

https://www.youtube.com/watch?v=7wM5EZ6JhFE

Centers for Disease Control and Prevention

Czeisler MÉ , Lane RI, Petrosky E, et al. Mental Health, Substance Use, and Suicidal Ideation During the COVID-19 Pandemic — United States, June 24–30, 2020. MMWR Morb Mortal Wkly Rep 2020;69:1049–1057. DOI: http://dx.doi.org/10.15585/mmwr.mm6932a1external icon

https://www.cdc.gov/mmwr/volumes/69/wr/mm6932a1.htm?s_cid=mm6932a1_w